ST. MUNGO

SOME NOTABLE GLASGOW STUDENTS DOWN THE CENTURIES

Glasgow, St. Mungo's 'dear green place', has grown over many centuries from a tiny settlement on the banks of a shallow stream to a major city with an international reputation in trade, commerce and engineering. Woven into this history is a long tradition of encouragement of learning and culture, notably through its ancient University, and now recognised by the accolade of European City of Culture, 1990. The University was the point of departure for many whose later lives helped shape the world we live in today. The brief histories of just some of them in these pages are offered as tribute both to them and to the City. By no means all of them are graduates; for most professions the possession of a formal degree was not required until well into this century and the mediaeval tradition of the wandering scholar was tenacious; but all of them attended classes in Glasgow University at some time. Some great Glasgow students are missing - David Livingstone, Lord Playfair and Lord Reith among them - for they properly belong to Glasgow's newer university, the University of Strathclyde. No living persons have been included, which is not to say that there are none living worthy of inclusion. In a hundred years' time there will doubtless be many more on the roll of honour of *St. Mungo's bairns.*

Carol Primrose

Glasgow University Library
1990

Acknowledgements

Our grateful thanks for help go to:-
Sheila Craik
Alice Crawford
Roger Hickman
Ronald Milne
Mary Sillito
of Glasgow University Library
and
Michael Moss
Lesley Richmond
of Glasgow University Archives

And for permission to reproduce illustrations to:-
Cameron Press
Collins Publishers
The Glasgow Herald
The Royal Free Hospital School of Medicine
The Scottish National Portrait Gallery
Scottish Television
Universal Pictorial

ISBN 085261 291 5

Printed by Shedden Macintosh, Clydebank

James Dalrymple (Viscount Stair) 1619-1695
Lawyer and Statesman M.A.1637

Viscount Stair (then James Dalrymple) studied Arts at Glasgow University, graduating M.A. in 1637. He went to Edinburgh to pursue a career in law, but became involved in the Civil War, commanding a troop in Glencairn's regiment. Invited to compete for appointment as Regent at Glasgow in 1641, he appeared at the examination still wearing the scarlet regimentals of a captain. As Regent he would teach Logic, Moral Philosophy, Politics and the elements of Mathematics , and he probably included a course in Jurisprudence, although Law was not taught formally in Glasgow at this time. One student who ever after remembered him with gratitude was John Snell, founder of the Snell Exhibitions.

Stair resigned as Regent in 1647 in order to embark on a legal career which raised him to President of the Court of Session in 1671. However, he was deprived of office on his refusal to take the oath required by the Test Act, fleeing to Holland to escape persecution. The advent of William of Orange in 1688 restored his fortunes; he was appointed Lord Advocate and reinstated as President of the Court of Session. Towards the end of his life he was accused of complicity in the treacherous massacre of the Macdonalds of Glencoe, although it seems probable that his son was more culpable than he. His domestic life was as turbulent as his public career; his wife was accused of witchcraft, his daughter's tragic marriage inspired Scott's *Bride of Lammermoor*, and his grandson was the instrument, albeit innocent, of his brother's death.

Stair's lasting claim to fame rests on his *Institutions of the Law of Scotland* (1681), the first and most authoritative comprehensive treatise of the subject, still today occasionally cited as a source of law. His reputation, other than as a jurist, is equivocal. Unquestionably, the man appointed to the Bench by Cromwell, knighted and created Baronet by Charles II, and raised to the Viscountcy by William of Orange must be accounted a very astute politician, but the very nature of the achievement casts doubt on his integrity. In the words of John Buchan, "his ability all men admitted, but few trusted him and fewer liked him. There was something uncanny about him and his race."

Robert Simson 1687-1768

Mathematician M.A.1711

Intended by his father for the ministry, Simson entered Glasgow University in 1702, and studied under his uncle John Simson, Professor of Divinity. He showed early distinction in Classics and Botany, but became attracted to mathematics and abandoned the idea of the church. After a further year's study in London, he was elected Professor of Mathematics at Glasgow in 1712.

In London, he had come under the influence of Edmund Halley, who reinforced his predilection for the ancient Greek writers, notably Euclid and Apollonius of Perga, for which his facility in classical languages suited him admirably. A major figure in the history of geometry, his edition of the *Elements* of Euclid, which first appeared in 1756, became the standard edition for a century, and still forms the basis of most modern textbooks. His 'restoration' of lost Greek treatises such as Euclid's *Porisms* and Apollonius's *Determinate Sections,* although necessarily conjectural and incomplete, clarified many problems of classical geometry. His antipathy to the algebraic treatment of conics and preference for "the purer models of antiquity" established synthetic rather than analytic geometry as the

dominant approach in British mathematics for many years.
  Described by Alexander Carlyle as a "master of all knowledge, even of theology", he was Clerk of Senate from 1728 to 1761. His eccentric habit of counting every footstep he took when out walking was relished as one of the local sights. A highly sociable man, in spite of a rooted aversion to the female sex, and not noted for temperance, he admitted "all and sundry to his symposia at a public house", where he demonstrated an improbable talent for singing classical Greek odes set to modern music.

Francis Hutcheson 1694-1746
Moral Philosopher

    The son of a Scottish dissenting minister who settled in Ireland, Hutcheson came to study Arts and Divinity at Glasgow University in 1710, where he met two men whose ideas shaped his later career. He absorbed the theology of John Simson (later tried for heresy by the Church of Scotland), to the distress of his father's congregation: "Your silly loon, Frank, has fashed a' the congregation wi' his idle cackle. He has been babbling this oor aboot a gude an' benevolent God, an' that the sauls o' the heathen themsels will gang tae Heeven if they follow the licht o' their ain consciences. Not a word does the daft boy ken, speir nor say aboot the gude, auld, comfortable doctrines o' election, reprobation, sin an' faith." Gershom Carmichael's wide-ranging and enquiring teaching of ethics, however, was even more influential in setting him on his true path.

    Returning to Ireland in 1720, he set up a Dissenting Academy in Dublin but devoted his free time to developing his ideas on ethics which were published in *An Inquiry into the Original of our Ideas of Beauty and Virtue* (1725) and *An Essay on the Nature and Conduct of the Passions and Affections with Illustrations upon the Moral Sense* (1728). After his election to the Chair of Moral Philosophy at Glasgow in 1729, he developed an anti-rationalist system of ethics (published after his death as *A Short Introduction to Moral Philosophy*) which posited a moral sense in man, not reason, as the foundation of morals. As a teacher he had what Alexander Carlyle described as "a fervent and persuasive eloquence that was irresistible", assisted perhaps by his revolutionary innovation of discussing topics generally, in English, instead of following the traditional method of giving oral commentary on a set text, in Latin.

A major figure in the history of philosophy, as a utilitarian he prefigured J.S. Mill and is credited as the originator of the concept of 'the greatest happiness of the greatest number'; in political economy his ideas on, for example, the advantages of the division of labour, and the theory of value, were taken up by his student, Adam Smith; a friend and mentor of David Hume, his views also helped shape the ideas of Thomas Reid, 'the father of Scottish philosophy'; so his was a seminal influence indeed.

William Cullen 1710-1790

Physician and Chemist M.D.1740

At an early age he attended classes in Arts at Glasgow, at the same time being apprenticed to a physician. In 1729, he took a post as surgeon on a merchant ship bound for the West Indies. On his return to London, he became assistant to an apothecary. Thus qualified in surgery and medicine, (a not uncommon route followed also by Smollett), he practised near Hamilton from 1731 to 1744, except for two sessions at Edinburgh Medical School, and gained an M.D. from Glasgow in 1740. From 1737 to 1740, his pupil and partner in the practice was William Hunter.

In 1744, he was appointed Lecturer in Materia Medica at Glasgow, and succeeded in having Chemistry established as a separate lectureship in 1746. He became Professor of Medicine in 1751, transferring to Edinburgh and occupying successively the Chairs of Chemistry (1755), Institutes of Medicine (1766) and Practice of Physic (1773). He was made a Fellow of the Royal Society in 1777.

At Glasgow, some of his discoveries on heat, and on the cooling of solutions, were developed by his pupil and close friend Joseph Black in his work on latent heat. Of Cullen's works, the two most important were the

Nosology (1769) and the *First Lines on the Practice of Physic* (1786). He recognised the difference between primary and secondary fevers, and attacked the concept of 'humours' as the causes of disease. He clearly separated symptoms from the diseases themselves, and recognised the inadequacy of contemporary treatment to attack the root of infections, distinguishing also between the effects of remedies and the natural healing powers of the body itself.

He was the first medical teacher at Glasgow to lecture in English, and his lectures were clear, well-illustrated and inspiring. Devoted to his students and his patients, (his only recreation was a weekly game of whist), he was generous with his time and his money; when he died just five weeks after retiring, he had virtually nothing in his estate. Though he made no outstanding discoveries, his capacity for clear perception, reasoning and judgement, coupled with his genius as a teacher, have brought him recognition as one of the leading British physicians of the eighteenth century.

William Hunter 1718-1783

Anatomist and Obstetrician M.D.1750

Hunter was intended for the Church, but while at Glasgow University from 1731 to 1736 the philosophical teachings of Francis Hutcheson turned him against the rigid dogmas of Presbyterian theology. An acquaintance with the physician William Cullen disposed him to the medical profession, and he studied with Cullen for three years. Eager to widen his experience, he went to London in 1741 with introductions to William Smellie and James Douglas, who fostered his interests in obstetrics and gynaecology respectively.

His career prospered; already by 1743 he had communicated the first of several papers to the Royal Society - *On the Structure and Diseases of Articulating Cartilage*, and in 1750 he was awarded an M.D. by Glasgow University. From the first, he had particularly interested himself in obstetrics, and in 1762 he was called to attend Queen Charlotte on the birth of her first child. Appointment as Physician Extraordinary to the Queen followed two years later, and Hunter rapidly became the most sought after physician in London.

His research, embodied in his *Anatomical Description of the*

Human Gravid Uterus which appeared in 1774, and his practical example, including the establishment of specialist training for both physicians and midwives, did much to establish obstetrics as a respectable branch of medicine for the first time, though he took a perverse pleasure in continuing to describe himself as a despised 'man-midwife'. However, he continued to lecture on surgical and anatomical topics also, with great success, being described as "admirably clear in exposition, and very attractive by reason of his stores of apposite anecdotes".

In private life he was a man of wide learning and artistic sensibilities and devoted many years to assembling a magnificent collection of books and manuscripts, coins, antiquities and works of art; these, with his working collection of anatomical and other specimens, were bequeathed to Glasgow University on his death. Generous to his friends, sensitive and sympathetic to his patients regardless of their degree, he was yet jealous of his reputation and prone to controversy, although he recognised his failing, pleading in mitigation that it was an occupational hazard for an anatomist, since corpses never answer back.

Tobias George Smollett 1721-1771

Novelist

Smollett attended Glasgow University for some time between 1735 and 1739, at the same time working first in a dispensary, then in 1736 as apprentice to a Glasgow surgeon. According to Walter Scott, he was at this time a scruffy, mischievous lad given to attacking what he saw as hypocrisy and humbug with satirical verses, and sometimes more solid missiles, behaviour which apparently commended him to his master, John Gordon, who preferred his "ain bubbly-nosed callant, wi' the stane in his pooch" to more sober-sided students.

Released from his apprenticeship in 1739, he went to London to pursue a medical career, but probably harbouring literary ambitions besides. Naval service from 1740 to 1741 as surgeon's mate on the expedition to Carthagena provided him with memorable raw material for his later novels, but by 1744 he was settled back in London practising as a surgeon.

His first novel, *Roderick Random*, appeared in 1748 achieving considerable success, as did *Peregrine Pickle* in 1751, but the later ones were less well received; Smollett's increasing depression, disillusionment

and splenetic rage against the iniquities of the society of his day seem to be paralleled in his writing. He involved himself in journalism which offered him scope for savage satire, though it also landed him in the King's Bench Prison for several months for libel.

A breakdown in health forced him to spend his final years abroad. But he continued to write, and regained his mental balance as his physical powers faded. His last work, *Humphrey Clinker*, demonstrates all his old brilliance of high comedy, acutely observed detail and memorable characterisation, but suffused with humanity and warmth. For a few short weeks before his death, he once again enjoyed critical and public acclaim.

Gavin Hamilton 1723-1798

Artist and Antiquarian

Unusually for a painter of this period Gavin Hamilton had a University education, studying at Glasgow from 1738 to 1742. Shortly thereafter, he seems to have gone to Rome, where he had lessons in painting from Agostino Masucci. He returned to Britain for some years, and in 1755 was one of the committee of artists responsible for founding the Royal Academy.

Initially, he devoted himself to portrait painting, achieving some fame in this area, but his profound interest in the Classics, and especially in Homer, led him to concentrate on paintings based on classical subjects. Most of his original paintings have been lost, and are known only from the many engravings made from them, but this evidence is sufficient to support the claim that he was the most important British painter in the neo-classical style. He was the first to adopt the severely classical ideal propounded by Winckelmann, and his densely populated but austere canvases anticipated the French master of the genre, David.

His fascination with the ideas of classical art drew him to the originals, in pursuit of which he excavated many Roman sites, including Antoninus Pius' villa, and that of Hadrian at Tivoli, which latter yielded the Warwick Vase now in the Burrell Collection in Glasgow. Although the works of art which he uncovered were carried off and sold to collectors, by contemporary standards he was a highly reputable antiquarian, if not above a little judicious 'restoration'.

His contemporaries admired him, not just as an artist, but as a man who was in the words of Fuseli "liberal and humane". Later in life he returned to Scotland with a view to settling permanently, but he found the climate too harsh after his years in Italy, and lived out his final days in Rome.

Adam Smith 1723-1790

Economist and Philosopher

Kirkcaldy, his birthplace in 1723, although a small town, had a bustling commercial life with collieries, salt pans, nail-making and shipping, besides its setting in an important agricultural area; so the young Adam Smith had an early practical introduction to one of his main interests of later years.

At fourteen years of age he entered Glasgow University, where he was greatly influenced by Francis Hutcheson. In 1744 he won the Snell Exhibition to Oxford where, however, he felt he learned little. Elected Professor of Logic at Glasgow in 1751, he transferred to the Chair of Moral Philosophy the following year, holding it for thirteen years - "by far the most useful and therefore as by far the happiest and most honourable period of my life". The city at this time was a thriving mercantile centre with the Tobacco Lords at the apex of its society, in whose clubs and coffee-houses he was able to cultivate the acquaintance of men of business, and test his ideas against practical experience.

In 1764, he resigned his chair to become Tutor to the Duke of Buccleugh on the Grand Tour, a much more lucrative post which, besides giving him a pension for life, enabled him to meet all the notables of Europe, including Voltaire. With another acquaintance, Samuel Johnson, he discussed the philosophy of Hume, although the outcome of the conversation was not perhaps in the highest philosophical strain. Johnson: "You, Sir, are a rogue". Smith: "And you, Sir, are the son of a _____".

He returned to Kirkcaldy in 1767 to concentrate on his writing. Late in life he became Commissioner of Customs for Scotland, and was Rector of Glasgow University from 1787 to 1789. Despite being perfectly capable of running his own and University affairs, he was notoriously absent-minded and inattentive to his surroundings, almost coming to a premature end for example when, showing a friend the operations of a tannery, he contrived to fall into the tanning pit.

His major work, *The Wealth of Nations* published in 1776, was immediately recognised as one of the seminal works in European philosophy, establishing political economy as a subject of study in its own right, and it remains influential up to the present day, although some latter-day interpretations have distorted his ideas. Smith was first and foremost a moral philosopher who initially established his reputation with *A Theory of Moral Sentiments* in 1759, and an insistence on a framework of moral obligation underlies all his thinking.

John Anderson 1726-1796

Pioneer of Popular Education M.A.1775

To his students he was Jolly Jack Phosphorus, in allusion more perhaps to his fiery temperament, than to his scientific experiments. His career at Glasgow University was marked by recurrent strife with his colleagues, whom he castigated in his will.

At 19, he played an enthusiastic part in the defence of Stirling against the Jacobite Army in the '45 rebellion. In 1759, his military expertise was deployed on the fortification of Greenock against the French. But the British Army did not appreciate his recoilless field gun, a lack of vision not shared by the French Revolutionary Government which accepted it enthusiastically in 1791. While in France, Anderson further aided the spirit of liberty by devising an aerial bombardment of Germany with revolutionary pamphlets, using gas-filled paper balloons.

Professor of Oriental Languages, with French and Italian, from 1755, he transferred to the Chair of Natural Philosophy in 1757, where his work on a Newcomen engine gave James Watt the opportunity to invent the separate condenser, which transformed steam power into the driving force of the Industrial Revolution. He had extensive knowledge of Roman antiquities and his collection of altars and legionary stones from the Antonine Wall laid the foundation of the Hunterian Museum's collection.

As a teacher, he was entertaining and innovatory, most notably in his introduction of evening classes in popular physics for working men. In his will, he left his estate to found 'Anderson's University' - to be a new kind of University, covering the whole range of science and literature; ladies were to be admitted, and evening classes offered on practical subjects. Among early students were 'Paraffin' Young, David Livingstone and Lord Playfair; one of the first professors was George Birkbeck, whose development of Anderson's ideas led to the establishment of the Mechanics' Institutes.

Anderson's University survived as a technical college until 1964, when it became Strathclyde University - a fitting memorial to a man ahead of his time.

Joseph Black 1728-1799

Chemist

Born in Bordeaux, where his father was a wine merchant, he came to Glasgow University in 1746. He studied chemistry under Cullen, and continued to work with him in his laboratory for three years, when he moved to Edinburgh to continue his studies, gaining an M.D. in 1754. Two years later he returned to Glasgow to succeed Cullen as Professor of Medicine and Lecturer in Chemistry, finally returning to Edinburgh in 1766 to occupy the Chair of Physics and Chemistry. He taught in English, illustrating his lectures by experiments, and gained such a reputation that it became fashionable to go and hear him. His demonstrations were striking; for example, he would decant 'fixed air' over a candle to extinguish it.

Chronic dyspepsia and bronchial problems which plagued him all his life may have been a factor in his choice of research, which took the form of a search for a milder alkali for medical application than the caustic remedies then in use. This led him to the discovery that magnesium carbonate discharges carbon dioxide ('fixed air') when treated with acid, revealing that a gas can exist in solid form in another body. His observation of the change of a complex compound into a simpler one led to the

discovery of oxygen, nitrogen and hydrogen, and laid the foundations of much of modern chemistry.

Between 1759 and 1763, his investigations into the quantity of heat required to raise the temperatures of different substances to the same level led to his discovery of latent heat, and established clearly the distinction between heat and temperature. He never published these researches, but discussed them with his students and with James Watt, who applied them to his work on condensers which enormously increased the efficiency of steam engines.

He published very little, and made no further serious contribution to chemical science. Poor health inhibited his work and he devoted much of his time and energies to its treatment; the efficacy of a diet of bread, prunes and watered milk may be questionable, but he did live to the age of seventy-one.

James Boswell 1740-1795

Biographer and Diarist

    Boswell began his university career at Edinburgh in 1753 and soon plunged into a life of hard drinking and riotous activity which included a passionate devotion to the theatre. To one of his intimates at this time, the actor-manager James Dance (Mr Love), posterity owes a debt since it was he who first encouraged Boswell to keep a diary. Another intimate friendship, with an actress, proved the last straw for Boswell's irate father, who removed him to Glasgow in 1759. With no congenial distractions there, he perforce applied himself to his studies under Adam Smith among others.
    Admitted to the Scottish bar in 1762, he immediately went to London and achieved his ambition to meet Dr Johnson, countering the great man's notorious dislike of Scotsmen with his craven plea "I do indeed come from Scotland but I cannot help it". During 1764 and 1765 he made a leisurely tour of Europe in the course of which his lion-hunting skills brought him the acquaintance of Rousseau and Voltaire. In 1773, he and Johnson undertook their Scottish tour; among others they met Flora Macdonald who seems to have been a disappointment, being unheroically

"mild and well-bred". Publication of Boswell's *Journal of a Tour to the Hebrides* was delayed until 1785, since Johnson planned to publish his own account and frowned on competition. After Johnson's death, Boswell began work in earnest on his *magnum opus The Life of Dr. Johnson*, which appeared in 1791, and is recognised today as probably the finest biography in the English language. His *London Diaries,* discovered only this century, complement his literary work in their revelation of the man behind the public persona.

Boswell was a hugely complex character: a witty, convivial, charming man who was racked by depression and self-doubt; a place-seeker whose transparent openness and reckless tongue constantly undermined his ambitions; a rake and libertine who was ever a prey to remorse and guilt. He died disappointed in his hopes of greatness, apparently unaware of the greatness of his achievement.

Thomas Muir of Huntershill 1765-1799

Lawyer and Revolutionary M.A.1782

Muir's early vocation for the ministry was supplanted by a devotion to the law as a means of political reform. On becoming an advocate in 1787, he quickly became known as a radical champion of the oppressed, incurring the implacable hatred of the Lord Advocate, Robert Dundas and Lord Braxfield, Scotland's own hanging judge.

The hopes of reform inspired in Britain by the French Revolution took a strongly nationalist form in Scotland and Ireland, and Muir's enthusiastic support for the idea of an independent Scottish republic led to his being charged with sedition. During his absence in France, Dundas contrived to have him unjustly outlawed as a fugitive from justice. On his return to Scotland in 1793, he became the central figure in a series of show trials designed by Dundas and Braxfield to crush the reform movement, but his eloquence and demeanour at the trial gave him the status of a martyr, and his sentence of fourteen years' transportation merely strengthened the resolve of the reformers.

He contrived to escape from Botany Bay to America, on a ship reputedly sent on the personal instructions of George Washington, but fell

into the hands of the Spanish who sent him back to Spain as a spy. Off Cadiz, the ship was attacked by the British; in the ensuing battle, Muir suffered severe head injuries, but the disfigurement to his face did at least enable him to evade capture. He eventually gained sanctuary in France in 1798, where he was hailed as a 'hero of the Republic' and a 'martyr of liberty'. Although ill and partially blinded, his will to continue the fight for Scottish freedom was undiminished, but his physical strength was spent, and he died suddenly in January 1799.

Thomas Campbell 1777 - 1844
Poet

His father, a Glasgow tobacco merchant, was ruined by the American War, obliging Campbell to support himself by tutoring while at Glasgow University between 1791 and 1796.

In 1796 he began *The Pleasures of Hope*, a long discursive poem in heroic couplets in the manner of Pope, but suffused with Romantic and libertarian ideas. Published in 1799, it was a runaway success with the public, though less admired by other poets — Wordsworth, for example, apostrophizing it as "poetical indigestion"; it caught the spirit of its time but has failed to hold its place in critical esteem.

His songs of battle such as *Ye Mariners of England* and *Hohenlinden* have had more lasting appeal, although Campbell castigated the latter as "damned drum and trumpet lines" and only published it at Walter Scott's urging. He also wrote a number of historical poems mainly on Scottish themes - *Lochiel's Warning, Lord Ullin's Daughter*.

Although in public "a merry companion, overflowing with humour and anecdote" according to Leigh Hunt, he was plagued by ill-health and suffered from depression and alcoholism intensified by family tragedy. Incompetent at managing his affairs, and very slow in producing his poetry (constantly changing and rewriting), he was obliged to spend much of his time on literary hackwork and journalism, "this perpetual galley-slavery", in order to make ends meet.

In spite of this, he devoted both time and money to help the victims of suffering and oppression. He worked hard in the cause of Polish and German freedom, supported Catholic emancipation in Ireland and savaged America on slavery - "a curse and a crime, that cannot be too soon abolished". Passionately interested in education, he was a prime mover in the establishment of London University, and saw his election as Lord Rector of Glasgow University in 1826 as "the crowning honour of his life".

Though little read today, as a transitional figure between the formal rhetoric of the eighteenth century and the Romantic Revival Campbell has his place in the mainstream of English poetry, and influenced many poets greater than himself - Byron, Shelley, Browning, Hopkins and Whittier among them. He is buried in Poets' Corner, Westminster Abbey.

Thomas Graham 1805-1869

Chemist M.A.1824

The son of a wealthy Glasgow merchant, he took an Arts degree at Glasgow, and then enrolled in Divinity at his father's insistence. But Graham was already deeply committed to chemistry; he moved to Edinburgh ostensibly to continue in Divinity, but in fact enrolled in the Medical School. When his father learned of the deception, he was cut off without even the proverbial penny, after a furious row.

Now obliged to support himself, he turned to tutoring and journalism in Glasgow and Edinburgh. In 1830, he obtained the Chair of Chemistry at Anderson's University in Glasgow, which he held until elected Professor of Chemistry at University College, London in 1837. In 1855, he became Master of the Mint, where he introduced the bronze coinage still in use today. He was made a Fellow of the Royal Society in 1836, and founded the Chemical Society of London in 1841.

Most of his pioneering work on gas diffusion, phosphates, colloids and dialysis was done before he left Glasgow. His first paper, on the absorption of gases by liquids, appeared in 1826. In 1831, in a paper to the Royal Society of Edinburgh, he published his law of the diffusion of gases, challenging the then accepted corpuscular theory; and a major contribution on the constitution of acids and salts appeared in the *Transactions and Proceedings of the Royal Society* in 1833.

His notebooks and letters show a lifelong interest in the practical applications of science. In 1827, he was pondering Nitrification, Sulphuric Acid, Steam, Steam Engines - cylinder - piston, Steel Pens and the Miscibility of Gases. Long before the advent of Mae West, he had hit on the idea of 'The Marine Amulet, or Life-preserver' - a combination of tartaric acid and soda-bicarbonate which, on contact with water, would fill a bag with carbonic gas and allow the wearer to float. As late as 1862, he was considering "Mr Yorke's problem of the brandy cherries and your own (his sister's) preserved greengages" - apparently relating to the tendency of preserved fruit to wrinkle. He produced an explanation, but unfortunately no solution.

William Thomson (Lord Kelvin) 1824-1907

Physicist

Schooled at home by his father, latterly Professor of Mathematics at Glasgow, Kelvin's entry to the University in 1834 marked his first experience of formal education. Nonetheless, Kelvin (then William Thomson) won the Astronomy class prize and the University Medal for his *Essay on the Figure of the Earth,* besides excelling in Classics and Moral Philosophy. He published his first paper in his final year (on Fourier analysis), before going to Cambridge, where he rowed for the University, helped to found the Musical Society, and published several more papers. After a short spell in Paris, at the College de France, he was appointed Professor of Natural Philosophy in Glasgow at the age of twenty-two in 1846, holding the Chair for fifty-three years.

"The nonpareil scientist of the nineteenth century", Kelvin was master of both theoretical and experimental research. With Joule, he worked on heat, discovering the 'Joule-Kelvin effect' which provided the theoretical basis for refrigeration and heat-engines, going on to make a major contribution to thermodynamics and to develop the Kelvin scale of temperature in which the zero point is absolute zero. The study of

magnetism led him to develop the magnetic compass, while his work on electric currents and electro-static fields provided the basis for the first Transatlantic cable, and the improvement of various forms of electric measurement. (His own house in Professors' Square was reputedly the first in Glasgow to be lit by electric light).

Less happily, he became embroiled in one of the longest-running of scientific controversies, the age of the earth, arguing against the evolutionists' demand for a timescale of hundreds of millions of years. In this he was wrong, though his reasoning was impeccable within the limits of the physical laws known at the time.

His genius was universally recognised and admired, but it could be a mixed blessing to his students. Although an inspiring teacher to those who could follow him, his lectures often left the slower-witted baffled; at least one of his assistants, Mr Day, better appreciated the needs of the average student, hence the legend on the blackboard which greeted the newly knighted professor on his return from his investiture:

'Work while the Day is with us,
For the Knight cometh when no man can work.'

Sir Henry Campbell-Bannerman 1836-1908
Liberal Prime Minister 1905-1908

Entering Glasgow University in 1851, Henry Campbell completed his degree in Classics at Cambridge, before returning to work in the family drapery firm. A career in politics beckoned, however. Although his family were staunch Conservatives, the son took his own line, and in 1867 was returned as the Radical Liberal member for Stirling Burghs. In 1871, he was appointed Secretary at the War Office.

In that year also, he was bequeathed a handsome fortune by an uncle, Henry Bannerman, on condition that he adopted the surname Bannerman. He resented this demand somewhat, but being a practical man took the name and the fortune. His wife resented it rather more, and in fact insisted on remaining plain Mrs Campbell for a considerable time, thereby causing a certain confusion among the ranks of polite society.

In 1884, Campbell-Bannerman was appointed Chief Secretary for Ireland, a difficult and dangerous job in which his legendary *sang froid* stood him in good stead. He became convinced that Home Rule was the only solution to the Irish Question, but the Tories mobilised public fears and brought down the Liberal Government on the issue. (Logically, he accepted that by the same token Home Rule should be extended to Scotland and Wales also.) He was knighted in 1895. Following the crisis in South Africa precipitated by the Jameson Raid, the Liberals, in disarray, turned to him as leader in 1899. He contrived to hold the party together and, as Prime Minister after the Liberal landslide of 1905, achieved a settlement in South Africa.

Although never a charismatic politician, he was honest, resolute and forward-looking. He supported the call for female suffrage; in the face of rampant jingoism, he denounced the "methods of barbarism" which had plunged the country into the Boer War; and, had he been able to achieve his settlement in Ireland, much bitterness and bloodshed in this century might have been averted.

David Murray 1842-1928

Lawyer, Antiquarian, Bibliographer M.A.1863

Murray came up to Glasgow University in 1858 and in a very real sense never left it thereafter. Always devoted to its interests, he was Rector's Assessor (1896-1899) and General Council Assessor to the Court from 1903 until his death. He adopted the legal profession, becoming senior partner in the firm of Maclay, Murray and Spens, and Dean of the Faculty of Procurators from 1895 to 1898, though a certain 'forcible bluntness' did not always endear him to his colleagues.

He began a lifelong habit of book collecting at the age of eight, eventually amassing a library of 14,000 volumes, including more than 1000 examples of early Glasgow printing, files of early Scottish periodicals, early school books, and early works on arithmetic and law, a magnificent collection which was bequeathed to the University Library at his death. The amazingly wide range of his interests is reflected both in his library and in his published works - books, pamphlets and periodical articles. He wrote on Scottish life and history, especially that of Glasgow, geology, law, museums, archaeology and contemporary political and social issues besides much else, sometimes doing battle for cherished ideas - fighting

against the removal of Glasgow's Register of Sasines to Edinburgh, pressing for free public libraries, and saving the University's Hunterian coin collection from dispersal in the teeth of opposition from the University itself. His plea for an archaeological survey of Scotland led to the establishment of the Royal Commission on the Ancient and Historical Monuments of Scotland.

In 1870, the University moved from its long-time home in the High Street to Gilmorehill; a request to Murray for a volume of reminiscences gave birth to his *magnum opus - Memories of the Old College of Glasgow.* As the *Glasgow Herald* reviewer pointed out, these memories were "to a very large extent ante natal" ranging from the foundation of the University in 1451 up to the ceremonial 'flitting' in 1870, and discussing its buildings, classes, professors and students in a clear engaging style incorporating a wealth of anecdote which brings the Old College to vibrant life.

As befitted a man who lived much in the past, Murray had an innate conservatism which he sometimes mobilised to frustrate change. But his was not a blinkered mind; he long advocated reform and simplification of his own legal specialism, conveyancing; he was a lifelong supporter of votes for women; and as early as 1894 was pressing the claims of 'Women as Lawyers'. Nor was this last mere empty words; his own firm was the first to admit a woman law apprentice, in 1917.

Andrew Lang 1844-1912

Folklorist, Writer and Journalist

Lang spent most of his undergraduate career at St. Andrews, but transferred to Glasgow for his final year in 1863 with "the sole and purely mercenary object" of winning the Snell Exhibition to Balliol College, Oxford. He hated his "undesirable exile" in Glasgow, with its "blackness, dirt, smoke" and "small, airless, crowded rooms". Despite his sufferings, however, he did win the Snell in 1864 and departed for the more congenial air of Oxford.

He spent eleven years at Oxford, as student and Fellow of Merton College, thereafter earning his living entirely by writing. His first book, published in 1872, was *Ballads and Lyrics of Old France, and Other Poems*, and by 1874 he was well embarked on a long career as a journalist, writing book reviews, occasional pieces and a series of leaders in the *Daily News* which were described by a contemporary as "like fairy tales written by an erudite Puck". A childhood interest in folk tales developed into one of the engrossing themes of his life. One outcome was the series of fairy tales for children beginning with *The Blue Fairy Book* of 1889, but, in a more academic vein, his refutation of Muller's 'Aryan' theories of the origin of myth was a solid contribution to anthropology. His range was wide: translations from the Classics and from Old French, a history of Scotland, biographies, historical romances, parodies. As a literary critic he was respected, though scorned by the consciously 'artistic' school for 'writing down' to the ordinary reader; with more justice, he was accused of a lack of sympathy with modern writers, although he appreciated H.G.Wells and even *The House with the Green Shutters*.

All his work is marked by wit, elegance and lightness of touch, but his underlying melancholy, his aestheticism and his distaste for sordid realism put him essentially at odds with life, from which he always longed to escape into a dream world of romance. Small wonder he felt an alien in the harsh realities of industrial Glasgow.

Sir William Macewen 1848-1924

Surgeon

Born on the Island of Bute, he had an idyllic childhood which instilled in him a lifelong love of nature and the sea. Watching and helping the local boatbuilders gave him a manual dexterity and a knowledge of techniques for manipulating rigid materials which he put to good use later in life. In 1865 he went to Glasgow University where he studied medicine under Lister. As a new student on the wards of the Royal Infirmary, the smell of putrifying flesh made him faint. He became Casualty Surgeon to the Central Police Office in 1871 and made some significant contributions to forensic science, notably his recognition of the symptomatic difference between alcoholic and other types of coma.

1873 saw the beginning of his work as a surgeon at the Western and Royal Infirmaries. He did revolutionary work on bone, facilitated by his recognition that bone grew from cells and not the periosteum, then the accepted wisdom. This enabled him to reconstruct shattered limbs and treat rickets, club foot and tubercular conditions using bone implants and transplants and fracturing and resetting bent bones (Macewen's Osteotomy). He developed an operation for radical mastoid through

'Macewen's Triangle', did pioneering work on the spinal chord and was the first surgeon to operate on the brain after locating the affected area from the physical signs, in 1879. He was also first to remove a lung successfully, in 1895; the patient subsequently took up open air preaching, to the surgeon's dismay. He emphasised the importance of patient care and stressed the value of the nurse's role. Lister had introduced him to antisepsis, but he realised the more significant concept of asepsis, insisting on sterile gowns and masks, scrubbed hands and properly sterilised instruments. Lister still wore the traditional frock coat and would happily use a scalpel picked up from the floor.
    'The man in the white coat' could be autocratic and intolerant of views contrary to his own; he drove others hard but was himself driven by an impulse encapsulated by his reaction to a stalking expedition; refusing to kill his stag, he said "my life has been to save life, not to destroy it".

James George Frazer 1854-1941

Anthropologist, Folklorist and Classical Scholar M.A.1874

Entering Glasgow University in 1869, he concentrated on Classics but also won a prize for mathematics, and was much influenced by Kelvin who introduced him to the concept of the physical world as governed by exact and unchanging laws capable of description in mathematical formulae. He valued his time here highly - "it laid the foundation of my whole subsequent career". He went to Trinity College, Cambridge in 1874, becoming a Fellow in 1879.

In Cambridge, he began work on a translation and commentary on Pausanias' *Description of Greece*, of the second century A.D. Originally intended as a short handbook for travellers, under his hand it grew to six volumes. The Greek original contains much comment on antiquities, religion and folklore, which seems to have kindled Frazer's interest. Articles for the *Encyclopaedia Britannica* on *Taboo* and *Totemism,* together with his friendship with William Robertson Smith, a Scottish biblical scholar and anthropologist, further developed his ideas on comparative anthropology as applied to religion. The outcome of these influences was *The Golden Bough* (1890), a study of the primitive mind and primitive religion, in which his extensive knowledge of classical writings gave him a very wide field of comparison. The book was hugely popular, with three editions in twenty-five years, each greatly expanded, and gained him Fellowship of the Royal Society, a knighthood and the Order of Merit.

Despite this success, his work was unscientific and out of touch. No traveller, his research was done in his library, and his theories based on reports by traders and missionaries. He compared examples from different places and periods without consideration of cultural significance. He ignored the implications of psychoanalysis and current sociological theory, and refused to read (far less learn from) critical reviews of his work. Nonetheless, although somewhat discredited as an anthropologist, his work still has value in the fields of comparative religion and classical literary criticism, and its literary power influenced a generation of ordinary readers to reassess their social and religious assumptions.

John Glaister 1856-1932

Forensic Scientist M.B.1879, M.D.1885

Glaister's interest in medicine was stimulated early when, at school in Lanark, he read the papers of a former pupil, William Smellie, the eighteenth century obstetrician who befriended William Hunter. Although he had been apprenticed to the law, the death of his parents in an epidemic when he was fifteen led to his uncle sending him to Glasgow University to study medicine. By a strange irony, Glaister himself and his wife died within hours of each other of influenza.

He completed the course in four years while still too young to sit the M.B. examination. A diploma from the Edinburgh Colleges enabled him to practise for two years, before taking his degree at the age of twenty-one. He established a practice in Townhead, then succeeded Macewen as lecturer in Medical Jurisprudence at the Royal Infirmary in 1881, becoming Professor in 1889 and moving to the University as Professor of Forensic Medicine and Public Health in 1899. He immediately set about modernising the department, establishing separate laboratories for each subject, using limelight slides and anecdotes from personal experience in his lectures, and providing a library and museum for the students.

In his role as an expert witness in criminal trials he became a household name, but his impact on the public imagination was as much due to his personality as his expertise. Though careful to keep abreast of developments in the field, in many cases his results were the outcome of careful observation and deduction rather than sophisticated scientific techniques. But he always had an air of supreme self-confidence in his own judgement, enhanced by his dramatic appearance and style and his use of down-to-earth non-technical language. This did not always operate in the interests of justice, as in the Oscar Slater case where his medical evidence, which provided the only link between Slater and the murdered woman, was quite unjustifiable as a basis for conviction.

He published the first edition of his *Medical Jurisprudence* in 1902; it was notable for its clear exposition, the highlighting of the differences between English and Scottish law, the inclusion of methods of criminal identification (particularly fingerprints) and especially for its photographic illustrations including microphotography. It is still today a standard textbook, in its 13th edition.

Marion Gilchrist 1864-1952

First Woman Graduate of Glasgow University M.B.,C.M.1894

She was educated at Hamilton Academy and attended advanced classes there between 1885 and 1890, gaining an LL.A. from St. Andrews University. Thereafter she took classes in medicine at Queen Margaret College in Glasgow from 1890, graduating M.B., C.M. with high commendation in 1894, the first woman to *graduate* in medicine in Scotland. In later years she recalled some of the difficulties: there was nowhere in or near the College where the women could get meals, and the local landladies were most reluctant to take them in as lodgers; more fundamentally, the Royal Infirmary tried to restrict their right of access to the wards, and their fellow students (male) tried to have them banned from the University altogether on the grounds that they (the men) were embarrassed and disadvantaged by their presence. Youth, in the shape of the students, proved markedly more reactionary than the elders of the academic body.

After a spell as an assistant, she went into practice for herself and specialised in opthalmology. She became Assistant Opthalmic Surgeon at the Victoria Infirmary from 1914 to 1930, undertaking *all* the work of the eye department during the First World War. During her career, she was active in several professional bodies, notably the British Medical Association (becoming the first woman Chairman of the Glasgow division) and the Medical Women's Federation, and was one of the trustees of the Muirhead Trust concerned with promoting medical education for women.

In her early days she was an enthusiastic supporter of the women's suffrage movement, being a member of the Women's Social and Political Union, the Women's Freedom League and several other societies, and she continued to fight for women's rights after that battle was won. Writing in 1935, she recalled pressing Principal Macalister to make a Professorship open to women. In response to his ingenuous claim that "All the University Chairs are open, and have always been open, to women. The University is founded on that of Bologna, and all its Chairs were open to women", she commented "Surely, if the Chairs were open, the right of entry to wo-men students was open too. When were these rights allowed to lapse? Let women now guard the rights for which so many of us have fought."

Cosmo Gordon Lang 1864-1944
Archbishop of Canterbury M.A.1882

Born in Fyvie, Aberdeenshire where his father was Church of Scotland minister, he went to Glasgow University studying under Kelvin who, however, was unable to enlighten him in physics or mathematics. Edward Caird was more successful - he "did not merely introduce me to the great masters of thought. He made me *think* ". Intending to read law, he went to Oxford University where he was a founder member of the Dramatic Society and became President of the Union. By his own account, though his conversion to the Church of England was gradual and almost unnoticed, his call to the priesthood had the dramatic suddenness of St. Paul's revelation on the road to Damascus.

Ordained in 1890, he became a curate at Leeds Parish Church. 1893 saw him back in Oxford as Dean of Divinity at Magdalen until appointed Vicar of Portsea in Portsmouth in 1896, where a parishioner was deeply shocked to see him 'practising celibacy in the street' (a reference to the wearing of his cassock outside the church). In 1901 he became Suffragan Bishop of Stepney, moving to York as Archbishop in 1908, fortified by King Edward's advice - "to keep the parties in the Church

together and to prevent the clergy from wearing moustaches". The former injunction proved the more difficult to keep, as witnessed by the failure of the Revised Prayer Book to receive Parliamentary assent in 1928, the year which saw him translated to Canterbury.

    In 1935 he visited the General Assembly of the Church of Scotland, where he was welcomed by the Moderator, his brother Marshall Lang. He also went to Balmoral where the king spoke of "certain family troubles" - the first intimation of the Abdication crisis of the following year. Lang was unjustly accused of trying to influence the outcome, but it is true that his broadcast after the event was harsh and uncharitable enough towards Edward to antagonize public opinion. The advent of the War convinced him that a younger, fitter man was needed to lead the Church through the conflict, and he resigned in January, 1942, his last act as Archbishop being the Confirmation of the future queen, Princess Elizabeth.

Elizabeth Dorothea Chalmers Smith c.1872-1944
Militant Suffragette M.B.,C.M.1894

As Elizabeth Dorothea Lyness, she was one of the first class of women medical students at Queen Margaret College in Glasgow in 1890, graduating in 1894 and practising medicine in Glasgow until her marriage in 1899 to the Reverend William Chalmers Smith, Minister of Calton Parish Church.

A fervent supporter of the demand for votes for women, she became involved in militant protest in Glasgow and was a central figure in the 'Park Mansion Affair' of 1914, when she and Ethel Moorhead were caught in the act of setting fire to an empty house. Taken to Duke Street prison "'they gave considerable trouble to the prison officials" and went on hunger strike. Released pending trial, they both failed to appear at the appointed time and were hunted as fugitives. Mrs Smith was rearrested in Tignabruaich. The new trial was "a scene of indescribable disorder and confusion" according to *The Glasgow Herald*, with 'missiles' (apples in actual fact) being thrown at the judge. The two women were found guilty and sentenced to eight months' imprisonment.

In the aftermath of the ensuing scandal she and her husband were divorced, it being agreed that he would have custody of the sons of the marriage and she the daughters. To support them and herself, she returned to a career in medicine, holding posts in Glasgow's Public Health Department and the Outpatients' Department at the Glasgow Royal Samaritans' Hospital for Women until 1930. Thereafter she was in private practice in Dennistoun until her death.

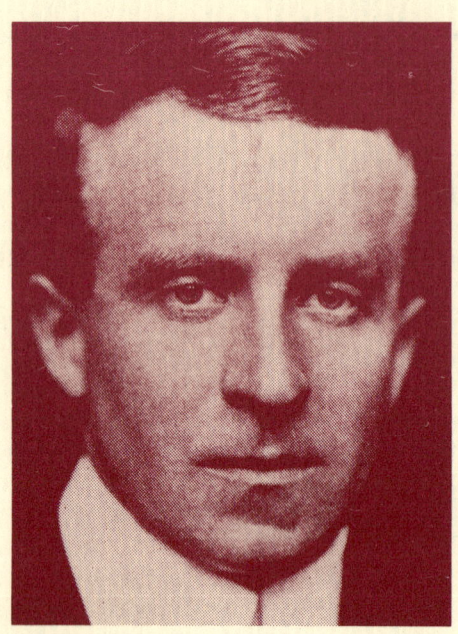

John Buchan (Baron Tweedsmuir) 1875-1940

Novelist and Administrator

He attended Glasgow University from 1892 to 1895, where he numbered among his teachers A.C. Bradley, Gilbert Murray and Lord Kelvin. Forty years later, he recalled that he "had to walk four miles through all varieties of unspeakable weather with which Glasgow, in winter, fortifies her children". He did battle in the Rectorial election where "I ... almost came by my end at the hands of a red-haired savage, one Robert Horne, who has since been Chancellor of the Exchequer", and contributed to the Glasgow University Magazine, revealing himself to be already the possessor of a mature command of English style. He left Glasgow on gaining an Oxford scholarship before completing his degree.

While at Oxford he became a reader for John Lane, recommending Arnold Bennett's first book for publication. He had already published his own first work, an edition of Bacon's Essays, before leaving Glasgow, and several more appeared during his Oxford years. He considered the Law as a profession, but in 1901 went with Milner to South Africa to help in reconstruction after the Boer War, one task being the dismantling of the notorious British concentration camps. His publishing activity resumed in

1906, on his appointment as a partner in Nelson.

The First World War saw him on the Western Front as a war correspondent for *The Times*, but by 1916 he was in the Intelligence Corps and a year later he became Director of the Department of Information. Appointment as Assistant Director of Reuters followed after the War, and at a by-election in 1927 he was elected Member of Parliament for the Scottish Universities. In 1935 he was created Baron Tweedsmuir on his appointment as Governor-General of Canada. He worked extremely hard, travelling widely even to the remotest Eskimo settlements. He loved the work and the country, his only regret being that the nature of his post restricted his public utterances to "Governor-Generalities".

Despite his active public life, he wrote continuously - histories, biographies, and the adventure novels for which he is best remembered, among them *Prester John, Greenmantle* and *The Thirty-nine Steps*. In all of them we can see the character of the man: possessed of the Roman virtues, gravity, piety and simplicity, but with a huge zest for life and adventure, and gifted with the rare skill of the story-teller.

Dame Anne Louise McIlroy 1878-1968

Pioneer of Women in Medicine M.B.,Ch.B.1898, M.D.1900, D.Sc.1910

One of Glasgow's first, and most distinguished, women medical graduates, she specialised in gynaecology and obstetrics, and became gynaecological surgeon at the Victoria Infirmary, Glasgow, from 1906-1910.

During the First World War, she commanded a unit of the Scottish Women's Hospitals serving in France, and then for three years in Salonika, and was surgeon in the Royal Army Medical Corps at Constantinople. She was responsible for setting up the Eastern Army's only orthopaedic centre, and established a school of nursing for Serbian girls. Among many honours, she received the French *Medaille des Epidemies*, the *Croix de Guerre avec Palme* and the *Serbian Order of St. Sava* and *Red Cross*. She describes these experiences in her book, *From a Balcony on the Bosphorus*.

In 1921, she was appointed the first woman Professor of Obstetrics and Gynaecology at London University, working at the Royal Free and other London hospitals. She was created D.B.E. in 1929, and in the same year became a founder Fellow of the Royal College of Obstetrics and Gynaecology. Later, she practised in Harley Street, becoming a Fellow of the Royal College of Physicians in 1937. In her sixties, she was again active in war work, organising emergency maternity services in Buckinghamshire.

She had great personal charm, and was both a brilliant speaker and an inspiring teacher. She was one of the first in the field to insist on the provision of anaesthetic as standard for maternity cases, to work on perinatal resuscitation, and to preach against "meddlesome midwifery".

Catherine Carswell 1879-1946

Novelist and Biographer

Born Catherine Macfarlane, she attended classes in English Literature at Glasgow University, becoming a friend as well as a pupil of Sir Walter Raleigh, but never actually matriculated as a student , although the University was open to women from 1892. Thereafter she studied music at Frankfurt.

Her first marriage, to Herbert Jackson in 1904, was ill-starred - he tried to kill her in a fit of insanity and was committed to an asylum for life. She made legal history when she won her case for annulment of the marriage. Returning to Glasgow for the birth of her daughter, she worked as a drama and literary critic for *The Glasgow Herald*. A favourable review of *The White Peacock* led to a close and lasting friendship with D.H. Lawrence, each becoming a trusted critic of the other's work. Lawrence pulled no punches: "You very often have a simply *beastly* style, indirect and roundabout and stiff-kneed and stupid ... But it is fascinatingly interesting. Nearly all of it is *marvellously* good".

1915 was an eventful year: she began work on her first novel *Open the Door,* which was published in 1920 winning the Melrose prize, she was sacked for a review praising *The Rainbow,* and she married for the second time, an enduringly happy union with Donald Carswell. Her second novel, *The Camomile,* appeared in 1922. Thereafter she concentrated on biography. *The Life of Robert Burns,* in which she attacked the sentimental, idealized view of the poet then current in an attempt to reveal the real man, made her well-known but also generated much hostile criticism. In 1932 appeared *The Savage Pilgrimage: a Narrative of D.H. Lawrence,* and in 1937 *The Tranquil Heart: a Portrait of Giovanni Boccaccio.* Her autobiography, *Lying Awake,* was published unfinished by her son in 1952.

In a sense all her work is autobiographical, concerned with the moral imperative of being true to oneself without regard to comfort or convention. Lawrence pinpointed this quality: "You are the only woman I have ever met who is so intrinsically detached, so essentially separate and isolated as to be a real artist and recorder". She herself put it rather differently: "I was *meant* ... perhaps to be a child and an old woman. I did my best in between, but in age the ecstasy returns without the agony, though it is not forgotten"

John Boyd Orr (Baron Boyd Orr of Brechin) 1880-1971

Nutritionist M.A.1902, M.D.1910

After education in the village school in Kilmaurs as pupil and pupil-teacher, he took an M.A. at Glasgow and became a teacher for three years. But he found, as others have done before and since, that though he liked the children he hated teaching them, so he returned to Glasgow University to take a degree in medicine and science. After a brief spell in general practice, he undertook research into diseases of malnutrition, stimulated by the revelation of the conditions of life of the slum children he had taught.

In 1914, he accepted a post as head of research in animal nutrition at Aberdeen, but almost immediately joined the R.A.M.C., gaining an M.C. at the Somme, a D.S.O. at Passchendaele, and a jaundiced view of the mentality of the regular Army officer, which led him to join the Royal Navy in 1918. However, he found himself seconded back to the Army to work on food requirement planning, thus becoming entitled to wear either military or naval uniform, a distinction he shared only with the King.

He returned to Aberdeen in 1918, to build up the Rowett Research Institute from nothing to a major research organisation publishing its own journal *Nutrition Abstracts and Views.* From this base he argued the urgent necessity of action to improve the diet of the poor. In the face of fierce governmental opposition, he produced the *Food, Health and Income Report* (1933-4) which showed that nearly half the population could not afford an adequate diet. During the Second World War he drew up a food plan which produced a better nourished population, in spite of rationing, than ever before.

   In 1945, he became the first Director-General of the Food and Agriculture Organisation of the United Nations, and tried in vain to establish a World Food Policy which would banish the worst inequalities, although his work was recognised in 1949 with the award of the Nobel Peace Prize. At various times he was a Member of Parliament, and after his public service, became a successful banker and farmer. He was made Companion of Honour in 1968, and became Chancellor of Glasgow University. Raised to the Peerage in 1948, he took the title Baron Boyd Orr of Brechin, though a friend suggested that 'Lord Orr Else' would have been more appropriate in view of his lifelong battles with intransigent authority.

George Farmer 1882-1965

Musicologist M.A.1924, Ph.D.1926

His earliest ambition, to be a military bandsman, he achieved at the age of 14, playing violin, clarinet and horn. In 1904, *Memoirs of the R.A. Band* marked his debut as musicologist in the first of his areas of expertise, military music. He left the army in 1910, ostensibly because a hernia prevented his playing the French horn, but his political and Freethinking views were probably equally disabling.

Musical directorships in the theatre followed, and in 1914 he came to the Empire Theatre in Glasgow, staying until 1947. During this period, he founded and conducted the Glasgow Symphony Orchestra (1919-1943), and was active in the Musicians' Union, editing *The Musicians' Journal* (1929-33) and founding the Scottish Musicians' Benevolent Fund in 1918.

His translation of Salvador-Daniel's 'La Musique Arabe' - *The Music and Musical Instruments of the Arab* (1915) - added Oriental music to his interests, and brought him to Glasgow University to study Oriental languages in pursuit of greater knowledge of Arabic sources. He became the acknowledged British authority on this subject and was offered a professorship at Cairo University, although he was unable to take it up.

While engaged in research, he continued to work in the theatre - "the only position of which I know, where I can earn a living with ample leisure for research and literary work". This leisure time activity ranged far beyond military and Oriental music: 1935 - *New Mozartiana,* 1947 - *History of Music in Scotland,* 1950 - *Handel's Kettledrums,* 1959 - *Bernard Shaw's Sister and her Friends,* and unpublished studies of Ernest Newman and the Paris Commune.

1951 saw him join Glasgow University Library to catalogue the Ewing Music Collection. His term as Keeper of Music, until 1965, brought the Library important collections of recent and contemporary Scottish composers' work, Mozart relics (including his last extant letter) and finally Farmer's own splendid collection of books and music.

Florence Marian McNeill 1886-1973

Author, Journalist, Broadcaster M.A.1912

After graduation from Glasgow University, she spent some time in Paris and the Rhineland studying art. An active, if law-abiding, suffragette, she organised the non-militant Scottish Federation of Women's Suffrage Societies.

She spent the years 1913-1917 in London as Secretary of the Association for Moral and Social Hygiene, a society founded by Josephine Butler, devoted to the care and protection of girls and young women. Her later work had a change of emphasis, but her continuing interest in social conditions was evidenced by her membership of the Secretary of State for Scotland's Advisory Committee on Rural Housing from 1944-5.

On her return to Scotland, she worked as a researcher for the Scottish National Dictionary, becoming Principal Assistant in 1929, and developing a deep interest in Scottish folklore and history, manifested in her writings. *The Scots Kitchen: its traditions and lore, with old-time recipes,* published in 1929, and still in print, was a pioneering study showing a fine awareness of the details of Scottish social history, and using her wide knowledge of Scots language and traditions to illustrate culinary history and its links with France. A complementary sequel, *The Scots Cellar,* followed in 1956.

Her major work was *The Silver Bough: a Study of the National and Local Festivals of Scotland,* published in four volumes between 1956 and 1970. A more personal sense of history led her to found the Clan MacNeil Association of Scotland in 1932. Inevitably perhaps, she supported the Scottish National Party, becoming a Vice-President in the 1930s.

In spite of the breadth of her interests and activities, she still found time for the recreations she listed as 'clarsach, ceilidh and kitchen' - a long life and a merry one.

John Logie Baird 1888-1946
Pioneer of Television

    Baird's inventive genius manifested itself early. While still at school he successfully installed electric lighting in his home with a home-made generator, and established a telephone exchange serving several neighbouring houses. A flying machine launched from the roof, however, was a spectacular failure, though the youthful pilot lived to invent again.

    After studying electrical engineering at the Royal Technical College, he took a six month intensive degree course at Glasgow University in 1914, though the advent of the War prevented its completion. Declared unfit for any war service, he set about trying to earn his living. His first project was the 'Baird undersock', which guaranteed dry feet in the wettest Scottish weather, and proved very successful, but a breakdown in health forced him to abandon it. Several other ventures, including 'Baird's Speedy Cleaner', had mixed fortunes before another bout of illness drove him to the south of England.

    There, in Hastings, he began his work on television in earnest. 1924 saw the first transmission of a moving image (a human hand), using a "seeing by wireless" machine constructed from a second-hand electric motor, a hatbox, a darning needle, a biscuit tin and a bicycle lamp. By 1928, he had devised Noctovision (a forerunner of radar), demonstrated colour television and recorded television pictures on wax and steel discs.

On the 30th September, 1929, the first experimental transmission from the BBC went out. Baird continued to refine his system and achieve new 'firsts' - he made the first outside broadcast (of the Derby) in 1931 - but the higher definition and more compact electronic system using the cathode ray tube was now in contention, and it was the latter which was adopted permanently by the BBC in 1937.

In spite of this crushing blow, Baird continued his work and during the Second World War devised an electronic system himself, giving high-definition, 3-dimensional colour pictures, but his sudden death in 1946 meant that it was never developed. The very fertility of his brain probably hindered him; his recurrent bouts of illness certainly did; but although today's television is not directly descended from his work, it was Baird's genius which brought television to birth and his vision and persistence which nurtured it.

James Bridie (Osborne Henry Mavor) 1888-1951
Dramatist M.B.,Ch.B.1913

Bridie (whose real name was O.H. Mavor) studied medicine at Glasgow from 1905-1913, in such time as he could spare from dominating the social life of the University. As editor of *Glasgow University Magazine,* he contributed drawings, light verse and stories in which he "solemnly tried to be funny", and he is also credited with responsibility for the University song, *Ygorra*. In December 1908, on the last day of term, he sat in the Students' Union and "roared for entertainment"; thus was born 'Daft Friday', religiously observed by every generation of Glasgow students since.

He qualified in 1913, joining the staff of the Royal Infirmary in Glasgow, but very soon found himself in the Royal Army Medical Corps during the First World War, serving in France and Mesopotamia. Years afterwards he remembered the eerie sensation of hearing the strains of *Ygorra* in the mud and desolation of Vimy Ridge. Returning to civilian life in 1919, he combined general practice with a post at the Victoria Infirmary, before obtaining the Chair of Medicine in Anderson's College in 1923.

His first play was *The Switchback*, although the first actually to be performed, in 1928, was *The Sunlight Sonata,* under the pseudonym Mary Henderson. Thereafter, Dr Mavor's *alter ego* Mr Bridie increasingly took over his life during the next twenty years to produce nearly forty plays, notably *The Anatomist, The Sleeping Clergyman, Mr Bolfry* and *Dr Angelus,* which were performed by such leading actors of the day as Edith Evans, Flora Robson, Laurence Olivier, Ralph Richardson, Alastair Sim and Duncan Macrae. Bridie was also co-founder of the Glasgow Citizens' Theatre in 1943, and of the College of Drama in Glasgow in 1950; with Tyrone Guthrie he was a moving spirit in the drama productions of the early Edinburgh Festivals.

    His plays are witty and entertaining, although much criticised for a lack of coherent structure and their startling mixture of farce and fantasy with conventional comedy and philosophical discursions. In fact, his technique was designed to explore the unresolved and unresolvable contradictions of good and evil in human life and was entirely appropriate to his purpose:- "all this nonsense about last acts. Only God can write last acts, and He seldom does. You should go out of the theatre with your head whirling with speculations".

Archibald Joseph Cronin 1896-1981

Novelist M.B.,Ch.B.1919, M.D.1925

    Cronin demonstrated a precocious talent for writing when, at the age of thirteen, he won a gold medal in a national competition for the best history essay, and English remained his favourite subject at school in Dumbarton Academy. Having been orphaned young, however, he needed a profession with a reliable income and opted for medicine when he came to Glasgow University in 1914. Although his studies were interrupted by the First World War, in which he served as a Surgeon-Sublieutenant in the Navy, he graduated as a doctor in 1919.

    After a short interlude as a ship's surgeon on a passenger liner bound for India, he held a range of hospital appointments between 1920 and 1921 in Glasgow, before becoming a general practitioner in South Wales. In 1924 he was appointed to the post of Medical Inspector of Mines. He gained his M.D. from Glasgow in 1925 for his thesis *A History of Aneurism*. Thereafter he established a busy medical practice in London's West End. Health reasons compelled him to retire from this work in 1931, however, to convalesce on a farm near Inveraray.

    There he decided to indulge his long-held, though secret, ambition to write. In three months' frenetic activity, he produced *Hatter's Castle,* his intense and violent first novel. Sent to a publisher chosen at random, it was accepted and became immediately successful. Its reception emboldened him to devote the rest of his life to literature, interrupted only by his work in the United States of America for the Ministry of Information from 1941 to 1945. A stream of successful novels followed, notably *The Stars Look Down, The Citadel* and *The Keys of the Kingdom.* His short stories on the work of a Scottish country doctor were adapted for television as the classic and enormously popular *Dr Finlay's Casebook.*

Cronin was out of sympathy with the more experimental developments of the twentieth century novel; he wrote in a traditional style "to lighten, not to enlighten the world".

John Grierson 1898-1972

Film-maker M.A.1923 'The Father of the Documentary'

After war service in the Navy (for which he falsified his age), he studied at Glasgow University from 1919 to 1923, where the political turmoil of Red Clydeside helped to shape his socialist convictions. Thereafter a Rockefeller fellowship took him to the United States of America. In Hollywood, he met Chaplin, Von Sternberg and De Mille among many others, and found his initial interest in journalism waning in favour of film as the more immediate and arresting medium.

On his return to the United Kingdom in 1928, he joined the Empire Marketing Board to make films promoting trade; the most notable of these was *Drifters* which he contrived to suffuse with that "atmosphere of higher meaning" present for him in the drama of real life. A move to the G.P.O. Film Unit resulted in his most famous film, *Night Mail* whose poetic script by W.H. Auden and music by Benjamin Britten went far beyond the mechanical function of letter delivery to touch on human emotions of love and loneliness. The train travelled from south to north at his insistence, a homecoming for the exiled Scot; Grierson always claimed he could feel a bump on the line where it crossed the border.

In 1939 he founded the National Film Board of Canada, and after some initial resistance, set it on course for the imaginative and highly influential organisation it became. Back in Britain after the War, he turned his hand to commercial films, notably *You're Only Young Twice* (based on a Bridie play) and *The Brave Don't Cry*; then with Films of Scotland he made *Seawards the Great Ships* in 1961, which brought him an Oscar. Finally, he moved into television with the documentary series *This Wonderful World* for Scottish Television, which ran from 1957 to 1967.

Grierson worked tirelessly and expected the same commitment from those who worked with him, but such was his capacity for inspiring enthusiasm that he carried everyone with him. In the 1930s, a suspicious Government, fearful of his left-wing views, planted a Special Branch man in his office. In short order, the spy in the camp was converted, started helping out in the research department, and eventually married Grierson's secretary.

Duncan Macrae   1905-1967

Actor

Glasgow born and bred, but of Gaelic-speaking Highland stock, Macrae was early acquainted with the broad spectrum of Scottish character types which he recreated later to such telling effect on the stage. He studied engineering at Glasgow University from 1923 to 1926, making his stage debut in the 'College Pudding' students' review, then taught in Glasgow for 10 years. His career as a professional actor did not begin until 1943, though he had been active in the amateur theatre for many years.

Fiercely nationalistic, (he cited his recreation as "abomination of English domination"), his great achievements lay in Scottish roles in the Scottish theatre such as *Jamie the Saxt, The Warld's Wonder, Gog and Magog,* and most memorably his Flatterie in the 1948 Edinburgh Festival revival of *The Thrie Estaits.* But he also acted on the London stage and overseas, playing in Shakespeare, Chekhov and contemporary English plays such as *Loot.* He disliked films, but had occasional character roles as in *Tunes of Glory,* and television work included his delightful Para Handy in *The Vital Spark.* He helped to found the Citizens' Theatre in 1943, and was prominent in the actors' union Equity. Parallel with his career as a 'serious' actor was his contribution to the indigenous Scottish pantomime tradition, beginning with the Citizens' *The Tintock Cup*, drawing huge new audiences into the theatre.

Macrae combined the gifts of actor, clown and mime. His performances were always immensely energetic yet deeply thoughtful; he could be hilariously funny but frequently with an underlying hint of tragedy; a master of the speaking gesture and perfect timing, he also possessed in his voice a marvellous instrument of great flexibility and expressiveness. The public reaction when he lay dying after a brain haemorrhage convinced Robert Kemp that "he was the best-loved Scot of his generation". The newspapers issued weekly bulletins on his condition, and at his funeral hundreds lined the streets to pay their tribute to this "eccentric genius of an actor".

William Barclay 1907-1978

Religious Writer and Broadcaster M.A.1929, B.D.1932

Bred up in Motherwell, Barclay went to Glasgow University in 1925, where he excelled in English and Classics (despite his devotion to football and music halls), and graduated with first class honours in Classics in 1929. His vocation clear from the first, he went on to Trinity College to study Divinity, taking his B.D. in 1932. After a year's post-graduate study at Marburg, he became minister at Trinity Church in Renfrew. In 1946, he gave up the parish ministry with regret and some misgivings to take up a lectureship at the University in New Testament Language and Literature, eventually becoming Professor of Divinity and Biblical Criticism in 1963. One cherished responsibility of his academic life was the conducting of the Trinity College choir, and he continued to make time for "the delightful uncertainty of supporting Motherwell [Football Club]".

His long career as a writer encompassed articles and book reviews, especially in *British Weekly* and *The Expository Times,* and some sixty books, notably *The Daily Study Bible (New Testament).* The burning conviction of the need to speak to ordinary people in language they could understand informed all his work - "unless religion is contemporary it is nothing". This view led naturally to his involvement in *The New English Bible*; equally inevitably it fostered such less academically dignified ventures as 'the book of the film' from Zeffirelli's *Life of Christ,* and another *Life of Christ* in strip cartoons.

    The same impulse drew him to broadcasting; beginning on radio, in 1962 he embarked on the series of television lectures which made him a household name. The most improbable of television personalities - he had a craggy face, with a big nose and a prominent hearing aid, coupled with a harsh, gravelly voice - nevertheless he could discourse on the meaning of *Agape* for half an hour and hold a huge audience spellbound.

    No theologian, as he himself admitted, neither was he a great scholar (except perhaps in Hellenistic Greek), but he was a supremely gifted communicator, crossing barriers of race, creed and class to take his message of the love of God to the common man.

Helen McInnes 1907-1985

Novelist M.A.1929 'The Queen of Spy Writers'

After Hermitage School, Helensburgh and the Girls' High School, Glasgow, she entered Glasgow University in 1925, taking an M.A. in French and German. While a student, she played tennis for the University, took an active role in the annual Student Charities' Week festivities and worked part-time in the University Library cataloguing early printed books. On graduation, she chose to continue working with books in Glasgow University Library, Dunbarton County Library and University College, London, where she took a post-graduate course in librarianship.

In her first week at University she had met a second year student - Gilbert Highet, later a noted classical scholar - and married him in 1932, when he gained a post at St. John's College, Oxford. There she combined bringing up her son Keith with amateur dramatics and extensive European travel in the summer vacations, paid for by translating books from German.

In 1937, her husband was offered the post of Professor of Latin and Greek at Columbia University and they moved to New York in 1938. In 1939, she began her first serious attempts at novel-writing, although it was some time before she felt able to reveal the fact to anyone other than her husband.

Her writing career proper began in 1941, with the publication of *Above suspicion*, which immediately became a best-seller, and was subsequently filmed. All her later books were equally successful with the public, being translated into 22 languages, with several being transferred to the screen. The novels are highly regarded for the quality of the writing and the authentic settings combined with her acute understanding of current affairs.

John Wheatley (Lord Wheatley) 1908-1988

Lord Advocate, Lord Justice Clerk M.A.1928, LL.B.1930

Wheatley was born in the Shettleston district of Glasgow into a family of pronounced Socialist sympathies. His uncle, also John Wheatley, who became the first Labour Minister of Health, involved his nephew in the aims and activities of the Independent Labour Party from an early age. But, even without this stimulus, he believed that the poverty and squalor he saw around him as a child would have taken him down the same road. He studied at Glasgow University, but took very little part in either the sporting or political life, being already deeply involved in these activities at home, and out of sympathy with the more conservative tenor of his fellow students. He was manning a picket line during the General Strike when many of his classmates were driving trams as strike-breakers.

Called to the Scottish Bar in 1932, he gained something of a reputation as a radical and continued his interest in politics, fighting seats in Glasgow and Ayrshire unsuccessfully for Labour. After an interruption to his career, serving in the Royal Field Artillery during the Second World War, he was made Solicitor-General for Scotland in 1947, becoming Lord Advocate the same year (until 1951) and sitting in Parliament as Labour member for East Edinburgh (1947-1954). Thereafter he became Lord Justice Clerk, spending 31 years on the Bench in a career marked with some ironies; as a devout Catholic with religious and moral objections to divorce he had charge of the notorious Argyll divorce case; as a convinced abolitionist, he was called upon to pronounce the last death sentence in Scotland.

He chaired many Enquiries and Committees, most notably the Royal Commission on the Reform of Local Government in Scotland, 1966-1969, in which "we ... tried to expound a philosophy of local government and local democracy and to strengthen the grassroots", though not everyone would agree that the reduction of Glasgow and Edinburgh to districts and the creation of one region (Strathclyde), nearly as big as all the rest put together, was the best way to achieve that aim.

Alistair MacLean   1922-1987
Novelist M.A.1953

Born into a Gaelic-speaking family at Daviot, Inverness-shire, he attended Inverness Royal Academy and Hillhead High School in Glasgow. The Second World War forced him into an unhappy relationship with the Royal Navy in 1941. Released in 1946, he entered Glasgow University to study English. Problems deriving, in part at least, from the requirement to study Anglo-Saxon, delayed his graduation until 1953.
During this period he supported himself in a variety of jobs, among them working in the Post Office, street-sweeping and conducting pleasure-boat cruises on the Firth of Clyde; this last venture proved rather disastrous when engine-failure left the boat drifting helplessly, and the ex-Navyman suffered the ignominy of rescue by H.M. Coastguard.
In 1954, while teaching in Rutherglen, he entered a short story competition organised by *The Glasgow Herald,* and won first prize. Collins, the Glasgow publishing house, enquired if he had written anything else and was somewhat reluctantly offered a large, untidy, brown paper parcel which turned out to contain the manuscript of *H.M.S. Ulysses,* published in 1955, it sold 250,000 copies in three months.   A similar

success with *The Guns of Navarone* in 1957 persuaded him to abandon teaching and write full time.

He maintained that he wrote 'adventure stories', not novels, and their strength certainly lies in fast-moving action, complicated, suspenseful plots and exotic locales rather than their conventional characterisation and rather pedestrian prose style. But besides such tales as *South by Java Head* (1958), *Ice Station Zebra* (1963) and *Where Eagles Dare* (1967), he wrote a Western - *Breakheart Pass* (1974), biographies of T.E. Lawrence and Captain Cook, spy thrillers under the pseudonym Ian Stuart - *The Dark Crusader* (1961) and *The Satan Bug* (1962), and plays and screenplays. His books sold in millions and many were filmed, so much so that in terms of popular appeal he was undoubtedly one of the world's most successful writers.

Ronald David Laing 1927-1989

M.B.,Ch.B.1951
Psychiatrist and Guru of 'The Swinging Sixties'

His future interests were prefigured during his student days at Glasgow University, where he founded The Socratic Society in 1948, intended to bring together students in medicine and the humanities and promote cross-fertilisation between the two cultures - a gulf he had identified and tried to bridge before C.P. Snow made the idea a commonplace.

Already looking beyond accepted ideas in psychiatry as a student, once in practice he challenged the current attitudes to mental illness in a series of books including *The Divided Self* (1960), *The Self and Others* (1962) and *Sanity, Madness and the Family* (1964), whose central theme was the need to respect the rights of the mentally ill as individuals, and to try to understand the meaning of 'mad' behaviour. This was developed to an extreme position which denied that schizophrenia was a state of illness at all, and attributed psychotic behaviour to the repressive actions of parents and society at large, exemplified by drug treatment and incarceration in mental hospitals, although he later retracted these views

In consequence, his influence waned in the medical world in his later years, but he gained a huge popular reputation in the sixties, which was only enhanced by his forays into literary and philosophical fields with books such as *Reason and Violence: a Decade of Sartre's Philosophy, 1950-1960* (1964) and *Knots* (1970).

While his more radical theories may have been of doubtful validity, his stress on the importance of sympathetic listening, understanding and respect for the patient revolutionised the practice of modern therapy to the lasting benefit of the mentally ill.